WHAT EVERY POLITICIAN THINKS ABOUT APART FROM POWER

I0429479

WHAT EVERY POLITICIAN THINKS ABOUT APART FROM POWER

INTENTIONALLY BLANK

INTENTIONALLY BLANK

WHAT EVERY POLITICIAN THINKS ABOUT APART FROM POWER

INTENTIONALLY BLANK

WHAT EVERY POLITICIAN THINKS ABOUT APART FROM POWER

INTENTIONALLY BLANK

WHAT EVERY POLITICIAN THINKS ABOUT APART FROM POWER

INTENTIONALLY BLANK

WHAT EVERY POLITICIAN THINKS ABOUT APART FROM POWER

INTENTIONALLY BLANK

WHAT EVERY POLITICIAN THINKS ABOUT APART FROM POWER

INTENTIONALLY BLANK

WHAT EVERY POLITICIAN THINKS ABOUT APART FROM POWER

INTENTIONALLY BLANK

WHAT EVERY POLITICIAN THINKS ABOUT APART FROM POWER

INTENTIONALLY BLANK

WHAT EVERY POLITICIAN THINKS ABOUT APART FROM POWER

INTENTIONALLY BLANK

WHAT EVERY POLITICIAN THINKS ABOUT APART FROM POWER

INTENTIONALLY BLANK

INTENTIONALLY BLANK

WHAT EVERY POLITICIAN THINKS ABOUT APART FROM POWER

INTENTIONALLY BLANK

WHAT EVERY POLITICIAN THINKS ABOUT APART FROM POWER

INTENTIONALLY BLANK

INTENTIONALLY BLANK

WHAT EVERY POLITICIAN THINKS ABOUT APART FROM POWER

INTENTIONALLY BLANK

WHAT EVERY POLITICIAN THINKS ABOUT APART FROM POWER

INTENTIONALLY BLANK

WHAT EVERY POLITICIAN THINKS ABOUT APART FROM POWER

INTENTIONALLY BLANK

INTENTIONALLY BLANK

WHAT EVERY POLITICIAN THINKS ABOUT APART FROM POWER

INTENTIONALLY BLANK

INTENTIONALLY BLANK

WHAT EVERY POLITICIAN THINKS ABOUT APART FROM POWER

INTENTIONALLY BLANK

INTENTIONALLY BLANK

WHAT EVERY POLITICIAN THINKS ABOUT APART FROM POWER

INTENTIONALLY BLANK

WHAT EVERY POLITICIAN THINKS ABOUT APART FROM POWER

INTENTIONALLY BLANK

INTENTIONALLY BLANK

INTENTIONALLY BLANK

WHAT EVERY POLITICIAN THINKS ABOUT APART FROM POWER

INTENTIONALLY BLANK

WHAT EVERY POLITICIAN THINKS ABOUT APART FROM POWER

INTENTIONALLY BLANK

INTENTIONALLY BLANK

WHAT EVERY POLITICIAN THINKS ABOUT APART FROM POWER

INTENTIONALLY BLANK

INTENTIONALLY BLANK

WHAT EVERY POLITICIAN THINKS ABOUT APART FROM POWER

INTENTIONALLY BLANK

INTENTIONALLY BLANK

WHAT EVERY POLITICIAN THINKS ABOUT APART FROM POWER

INTENTIONALLY BLANK

WHAT EVERY POLITICIAN THINKS ABOUT APART FROM POWER

INTENTIONALLY BLANK

INTENTIONALLY BLANK

WHAT EVERY POLITICIAN THINKS ABOUT APART FROM POWER

INTENTIONALLY BLANK

INTENTIONALLY BLANK

WHAT EVERY POLITICIAN THINKS ABOUT APART FROM POWER

INTENTIONALLY BLANK

WHAT EVERY POLITICIAN THINKS ABOUT APART FROM POWER

INTENTIONALLY BLANK

INTENTIONALLY BLANK

WHAT EVERY POLITICIAN THINKS ABOUT APART FROM POWER

INTENTIONALLY BLANK

WHAT EVERY POLITICIAN THINKS ABOUT APART FROM POWER

INTENTIONALLY BLANK

INTENTIONALLY BLANK

INTENTIONALLY BLANK

WHAT EVERY POLITICIAN THINKS ABOUT APART FROM POWER

INTENTIONALLY BLANK

INTENTIONALLY BLANK

WHAT EVERY POLITICIAN THINKS ABOUT APART FROM POWER

INTENTIONALLY BLANK

INTENTIONALLY BLANK

WHAT EVERY POLITICIAN THINKS ABOUT APART FROM POWER

INTENTIONALLY BLANK

WHAT EVERY POLITICIAN THINKS ABOUT APART FROM POWER

INTENTIONALLY BLANK

INTENTIONALLY BLANK

WHAT EVERY POLITICIAN THINKS ABOUT APART FROM POWER

INTENTIONALLY BLANK

WHAT EVERY POLITICIAN THINKS ABOUT APART FROM POWER

INTENTIONALLY BLANK

WHAT EVERY POLITICIAN THINKS ABOUT APART FROM POWER

INTENTIONALLY BLANK

WHAT EVERY POLITICIAN THINKS ABOUT APART FROM POWER

INTENTIONALLY BLANK

WHAT EVERY POLITICIAN THINKS ABOUT APART FROM POWER

INTENTIONALLY BLANK

WHAT EVERY POLITICIAN THINKS ABOUT APART FROM POWER

WHAT EVERY POLITICIAN THINKS ABOUT APART FROM POWER

INTENTIONALLY BLANK

WHAT EVERY POLITICIAN THINKS ABOUT APART FROM POWER

INTENTIONALLY BLANK

WHAT EVERY POLITICIAN THINKS ABOUT APART FROM POWER

INTENTIONALLY BLANK

WHAT EVERY POLITICIAN THINKS ABOUT APART FROM POWER

INTENTIONALLY BLANK

WHAT EVERY POLITICIAN THINKS ABOUT APART FROM POWER

INTENTIONALLY BLANK

WHAT EVERY POLITICIAN THINKS ABOUT APART FROM POWER

INTENTIONALLY BLANK

WHAT EVERY POLITICIAN THINKS ABOUT APART FROM POWER

INTENTIONALLY BLANK

WHAT EVERY POLITICIAN THINKS ABOUT APART FROM POWER

INTENTIONALLY BLANK

WHAT EVERY POLITICIAN THINKS ABOUT APART FROM POWER

INTENTIONALLY BLANK

INTENTIONALLY BLANK

WHAT EVERY POLITICIAN THINKS ABOUT APART FROM POWER

INTENTIONALLY BLANK

INTENTIONALLY BLANK

WHAT EVERY POLITICIAN THINKS ABOUT APART FROM POWER

INTENTIONALLY BLANK

WHAT EVERY POLITICIAN THINKS ABOUT APART FROM POWER

INTENTIONALLY BLANK

INTENTIONALLY BLANK

WHAT EVERY POLITICIAN THINKS ABOUT APART FROM POWER

INTENTIONALLY BLANK

INTENTIONALLY BLANK

WHAT EVERY POLITICIAN THINKS ABOUT APART FROM POWER

INTENTIONALLY BLANK

INTENTIONALLY BLANK

WHAT EVERY POLITICIAN THINKS ABOUT APART FROM POWER

INTENTIONALLY BLANK

WHAT EVERY POLITICIAN THINKS ABOUT APART FROM POWER

INTENTIONALLY BLANK

INTENTIONALLY BLANK

WHAT EVERY POLITICIAN THINKS ABOUT APART FROM POWER

INTENTIONALLY BLANK

INTENTIONALLY BLANK

WHAT EVERY POLITICIAN THINKS ABOUT APART FROM POWER

INTENTIONALLY BLANK

INTENTIONALLY BLANK

WHAT EVERY POLITICIAN THINKS ABOUT APART FROM POWER

INTENTIONALLY BLANK

WHAT EVERY POLITICIAN THINKS ABOUT APART FROM POWER

INTENTIONALLY BLANK

INTENTIONALLY BLANK

WHAT EVERY POLITICIAN THINKS ABOUT APART FROM POWER

INTENTIONALLY BLANK

INTENTIONALLY BLANK

WHAT EVERY POLITICIAN THINKS ABOUT APART FROM POWER

INTENTIONALLY BLANK

WHAT EVERY POLITICIAN THINKS ABOUT APART FROM POWER

INTENTIONALLY BLANK

WHAT EVERY POLITICIAN THINKS ABOUT APART FROM POWER

INTENTIONALLY BLANK

INTENTIONALLY BLANK

WHAT EVERY POLITICIAN THINKS ABOUT APART FROM POWER

INTENTIONALLY BLANK

WHAT EVERY POLITICIAN THINKS ABOUT APART FROM POWER

INTENTIONALLY BLANK

WHAT EVERY POLITICIAN THINKS ABOUT APART FROM POWER

INTENTIONALLY BLANK

WHAT EVERY POLITICIAN THINKS ABOUT APART FROM POWER

INTENTIONALLY BLANK

WHAT EVERY POLITICIAN THINKS ABOUT APART FROM POWER

INTENTIONALLY BLANK

WHAT EVERY POLITICIAN THINKS ABOUT APART FROM POWER

INTENTIONALLY BLANK

INTENTIONALLY BLANK

WHAT EVERY POLITICIAN THINKS ABOUT APART FROM POWER

INTENTIONALLY BLANK

WHAT EVERY POLITICIAN THINKS ABOUT APART FROM POWER

INTENTIONALLY BLANK

WHAT EVERY POLITICIAN THINKS ABOUT APART FROM POWER

INTENTIONALLY BLANK

WHAT EVERY POLITICIAN THINKS ABOUT APART FROM POWER

INTENTIONALLY BLANK

WHAT EVERY POLITICIAN THINKS ABOUT APART FROM POWER

INTENTIONALLY BLANK

INTENTIONALLY BLANK

WHAT EVERY POLITICIAN THINKS ABOUT APART FROM POWER

INTENTIONALLY BLANK

INTENTIONALLY BLANK

WHAT EVERY POLITICIAN THINKS ABOUT APART FROM POWER

INTENTIONALLY BLANK

INTENTIONALLY BLANK

WHAT EVERY POLITICIAN THINKS ABOUT APART FROM POWER

INTENTIONALLY BLANK

WHAT EVERY POLITICIAN THINKS ABOUT APART FROM POWER

INTENTIONALLY BLANK

WHAT EVERY POLITICIAN THINKS ABOUT APART FROM POWER

INTENTIONALLY BLANK

INTENTIONALLY BLANK

WHAT EVERY POLITICIAN THINKS ABOUT APART FROM POWER

INTENTIONALLY BLANK

INTENTIONALLY BLANK

INTENTIONALLY BLANK

INTENTIONALLY BLANK

WHAT EVERY POLITICIAN THINKS ABOUT APART FROM POWER

INTENTIONALLY BLANK

INTENTIONALLY BLANK

WHAT EVERY POLITICIAN THINKS ABOUT APART FROM POWER

INTENTIONALLY BLANK

WHAT EVERY POLITICIAN THINKS ABOUT APART FROM POWER

INTENTIONALLY BLANK

INTENTIONALLY BLANK

WHAT EVERY POLITICIAN THINKS ABOUT APART FROM POWER

INTENTIONALLY BLANK

INTENTIONALLY BLANK

WHAT EVERY POLITICIAN THINKS ABOUT APART FROM POWER

INTENTIONALLY BLANK

WHAT EVERY POLITICIAN THINKS ABOUT APART FROM POWER

INTENTIONALLY BLANK

INTENTIONALLY BLANK

WHAT EVERY POLITICIAN THINKS ABOUT APART FROM POWER

INTENTIONALLY BLANK

INTENTIONALLY BLANK

INTENTIONALLY BLANK

INTENTIONALLY BLANK

WHAT EVERY POLITICIAN THINKS ABOUT APART FROM POWER

INTENTIONALLY BLANK

WHAT EVERY POLITICIAN THINKS ABOUT APART FROM POWER

INTENTIONALLY BLANK

WHAT EVERY POLITICIAN THINKS ABOUT APART FROM POWER

INTENTIONALLY BLANK

WHAT EVERY POLITICIAN THINKS ABOUT APART FROM POWER

INTENTIONALLY BLANK

INTENTIONALLY BLANK

INTENTIONALLY BLANK

WHAT EVERY POLITICIAN THINKS ABOUT APART FROM POWER

INTENTIONALLY BLANK

INTENTIONALLY BLANK

WHAT EVERY POLITICIAN THINKS ABOUT APART FROM POWER

INTENTIONALLY BLANK

WHAT EVERY POLITICIAN THINKS ABOUT APART FROM POWER

INTENTIONALLY BLANK

WHAT EVERY POLITICIAN THINKS ABOUT APART FROM POWER

INTENTIONALLY BLANK

INTENTIONALLY BLANK

WHAT EVERY POLITICIAN THINKS ABOUT APART FROM POWER

INTENTIONALLY BLANK

WHAT EVERY POLITICIAN THINKS ABOUT APART FROM POWER

INTENTIONALLY BLANK

WHAT EVERY POLITICIAN THINKS ABOUT APART FROM POWER

INTENTIONALLY BLANK

WHAT EVERY POLITICIAN THINKS ABOUT APART FROM POWER

INTENTIONALLY BLANK

WHAT EVERY POLITICIAN THINKS ABOUT APART FROM POWER

INTENTIONALLY BLANK

WHAT EVERY POLITICIAN THINKS ABOUT APART FROM POWER

INTENTIONALLY BLANK

WHAT EVERY POLITICIAN THINKS ABOUT APART FROM POWER

INTENTIONALLY BLANK

WHAT EVERY POLITICIAN THINKS ABOUT APART FROM POWER

INTENTIONALLY BLANK

INTENTIONALLY BLANK

INTENTIONALLY BLANK

WHAT EVERY POLITICIAN THINKS ABOUT APART FROM POWER

INTENTIONALLY BLANK

INTENTIONALLY BLANK

WHAT EVERY POLITICIAN THINKS ABOUT APART FROM POWER

INTENTIONALLY BLANK

INTENTIONALLY BLANK

WHAT EVERY POLITICIAN THINKS ABOUT APART FROM POWER

INTENTIONALLY BLANK